LAUGH
-OUT-
LOUD
ANIMAL
JOKES
for
KIDS

Other Books by Rob Elliott

Knock-Knock Jokes for Kids
Laugh-Out-Loud Jokes for Kids
88 Great Daddy-Daughter Dates (as Rob Teigen,
with Joanna Teigen)

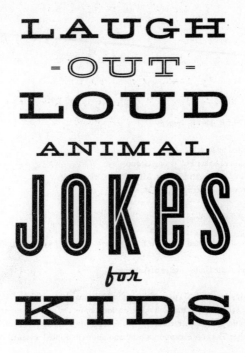

LAUGH -OUT- LOUD ANIMAL JOKES for KIDS

ROB ELLIOTT

SPIRE

© 2012 by Robert E. Teigen

Published by Revell
a division of Baker Publishing Group
P.O. Box 6287, Grand Rapids, MI 49516-6287
www.revellbooks.com

ISBN 978-0-8007-2375-0

Previously published under the title *Zoolarious Animal Jokes for Kids*

Printed in the United States of America

Scripture quotations are from The Holy Bible, English Standard Version®
(ESV®), copyright © 2001 by Crossway, a publishing ministry of Good News
Publishers. Used by permission. All rights reserved. ESV Text Edition: 2007

The poem "Ode to a Cricket" is used by permission.

The internet addresses, email addresses, and phone numbers in this book are
accurate at the time of publication. They are provided as a resource. Baker Publishing Group does not endorse them or vouch for their content or permanence.

18   19   20   21   14   13   12   11   10

I'd like to dedicate this book to my three older brothers, Tim, Scott, and Mark. They are really great brothers and friends, and it was a lot of fun growing up with them (most of the time!).

I'd also like to thank all of the kids who pick up and read *Laugh-Out-Loud Animal Jokes for Kids*. Your smiles and laughter mean so much to the people who care about you, so keep up the good work!

This book combines two of my favorite things: laughter and God's creation. I hope you enjoy reading the book as much as I enjoyed putting it together!

And God said, "Let the earth bring forth living creatures according to their kinds—livestock and creeping things and beasts of the earth according to their kinds." And it was so. And God made the beasts of the earth according to their kinds and the livestock according to their kinds, and everything that creeps on the ground according to its kind. And God saw that it was good.

Genesis 1:24-25

Q: Where do ants like to eat?
A: At a restaur-ant.

Q: What do alligators drink after they work out?
A: Gator-ade.

Q: What do a mouse and a wheel have in common?
A: They both squeak.

Q: What do frogs use so they can see better?
A: Frog-lights.

Q: Why can't you trust a pig?
A: It will always squeal on you.

Q: What kind of dog cries the most?
A: A Chi-wah-wah (Chihuahua).

Q: Where do birds invest their money?
A: In the stork market (stock market).

Q: Why can't you borrow money from a canary?
A: Because they're so cheep (cheap).

Q: What happened to the bee after he had four cups of coffee?
A: He got a buzz.

Q: Why was the bird nervous after lunch?
A: He had butterflies in his stomach.

Q: What did the father buffalo say to his son as he left for school?
A: "Bison (Bye, Son)."

Q: Where did the bat go to get some money?
A: The blood bank.

Q: What kind of bear doesn't have any teeth?
A: A gummy bear.

Q: What do you get from a pampered cow?
A: Spoiled milk.

Q: A cowboy arrives at the ranch on a Sunday, stays three days, and leaves on Friday. How is that possible?
A: His horse's name is Friday.

Q: How did the cow make some extra money?
A: By mooooo-nlighting at another farm.

Q: Why did the cow become an astronaut?
A: So it could walk on the moooo-n.

Did You Know · · ·

- Cows give an average of 2,000 gallons of milk per year. That's over 30,000 glasses of milk!

www.arsusda.gov

- There are about 11 million cows in America. They will make about 57.5 billion gallons of milk in a year.

www.umpquadairy.com

Q: What do cows like to eat?
A: Smoooothies.

Q: Why were the chickens so tired?
A: They were working around the cluck.

Q: What animals do you find in a monastery?
A: Chip-monks!

A duck walks into a store and asks the manager if he sells grapes. The manager says no, so the duck leaves. The next day the duck goes back to the store and asks the manager if he sells grapes. The manager says, "NO, we don't sell grapes," so the duck leaves the store. The next day the duck goes back to the same store and asks the manager if he sells grapes. The manager is furious now and says, "NO, WE DO NOT SELL GRAPES! IF YOU COME BACK AND ASK IF WE SELL GRAPES AGAIN, I'LL GLUE YOUR BEAK TO THE FLOOR!" The next day the duck goes back to the same store and says to the manager, "Excuse me, do you sell glue at this store?" The manager says, "No, we don't sell glue." The duck replies, "That's good. Do you sell grapes?"

Joe: Did that dolphin splash you by accident?
Bill: No, it was on porpoise!

Q: Why do flamingos stand on one leg?
A: If they lifted the other leg, they'd fall over.

Q: Where did the toy giraffe go when it was broken?
A: To get plastic surgery.

Q: What do you give a pig that has a cold?
A: Trough syrup!

Q: Why did the porcupine get sent home from the party?
A: He was popping all the balloons!

Q: What do you get when you cross a pig with a Christmas tree?
A: A pork-u-pine.

Q: What is a reptile's favorite movie?
A: The Lizard of Oz.

Q: What did the spider do with its new car?
A: It took it for a spin.

Q: Where do shrimp go if they need money?
A: The prawn shop.

Did You Know . . .
A shrimp's heart is located in its head.

Q: Why did the snake lose his case in court?
A: He didn't have a leg to stand on.

Q: What do you get when you cross a fish and a kitten?
A: A purr-anha.

Q: What kind of bull doesn't have horns?
A: A bullfrog.

Q: How are fish and music the same?
A: They both have scales.

Q: Why did the skunk have to stay in bed and take its medicine?
A: It was the doctor's odors.

Q: What did the mother lion say to her cubs before dinner?
A: "Shall we prey?"

Q: What's worse than raining cats and dogs?
A: Hailing taxi cabs.

Q: Why are pigs so bad at football?
A: They're always hogging the ball.

Q: What is a whale's favorite game?
A: Swallow the leader.

Q: Why are fish so bad at basketball?
A: They don't like getting close to the net.

Q: Where do dogs go if they lose their tails?
A: The re-tail store.

Q: What do you call a bear with no ears?
A: B.

Q: Why can't you trust what a baby chick says?
A: Talk is cheep.

Q: What are the funniest fish at the aquarium?
A: The clown fish.

Q: What is as big as an elephant but weighs zero pounds?
A: An elephant's shadow.

Q: Why are horses always so negative?
A: They say "neigh" (nay) to everything.

Q: What is black and white, black and white, black and white, black and white, splash?

A: A penguin rolling down an iceberg into the water.

Did You Know . . .

Penguins can jump up to 6 feet high.

Q: What is the smartest animal?
A: A snake, because no one can pull its leg.

Two men went deer hunting. One man asked the other, "Did you ever hunt bear?" The other hunter said, "No, but one time I went fishing in my shorts."

Q: What is the best way to communicate with a fish?
A: Drop it a line!

Q: Why couldn't the elephants go swimming at the pool?
A: They were always losing their trunks.

Q: Why did the robin go to the library?
A: It was looking for bookworms.

Q: What did the dog say when he rubbed sandpaper on his tail?
A: "Ruff, ruff!"

Q: What is black and white and red all over?
A: A penguin that's embarrassed.

Q: What do you call a pig that is no fun to be around?
A: A boar.

Q: What kind of fish can perform surgery?
A: Sturgeons.

Q: What kind of sea creature hates all the others?
A: A hermit crab.

Q: Where can you go to see mummies of cows?
A: The moo-seum of history.

Q: What kind of seafood tastes great with peanut butter?
A: Jellyfish.

Q: What do cats like to put in their milk?
A: Mice cubes.

Q: What do you get when you cross an elephant with a fish?
A: Swimming trunks.

Q: What do you do if your dog steals your spelling homework?
A: Take the words right out of his mouth.

Q: Why did the cat get detention at school?
A: Because he was a cheetah (cheater).

Q: Where do bees come from?
A: Sting-apore and Bee-livia.

Q: Why couldn't the polar bear get along with the penguin?
A: They were polar opposites.

Q: What did the rooster say to the hen?
A: "Don't count your chickens before they hatch."

Q: What did the whale say to the dolphin?
A: "Long time no sea (see)."

Q: What sound do porcupines make when they kiss?

A: Ouch!

Q: What happened when the frog's car broke down?

A: It had to be toad away (towed).

Q: What happens when a cat eats a lemon?

A: You get a sour-puss.

Q: How do you communicate with a pig?

A: Use swine language (sign).

Q: What do cars and elephants have in common?

A: They both have trunks.

Q: What is a whale's favorite candy?

A: Blubber gum.

Q: What is a bat's motto?
A: Hang in there!

Q: What do you get when you cross a rabbit and frog?
A: A bunny ribbit.

Q: What do you get when you cross a dog and a daisy?
A: A collie-flower.

Q: What does a cat say when it's surprised?
A: "Me-WOW."

Q: Why did the parakeet go to the candy store?
A: To get a tweet.

Q: What do you have if your dog can't bark?
A: A hush puppy.

Q: Why do seagulls fly over the sea?
A: If they flew over the bay they'd be bagels!

**Q: What do you get when you cross a cow and a
rabbit?**
A: You get hare in your milk.

Q: Why did the horse keep falling over?
A: It just wasn't stable.

Q: How do fish pay their bills?
A: With sand dollars.

**Q: Which creatures on Noah's ark didn't come in
pairs?**
A: The worms—they came in apples.

Q: How do you shoot a bumblebee?
A: With a bee-bee gun.

What Does the Bee Do?
Christina Rosetti

What does the bee do?
Bring home honey.
And what does Father do?
Bring home money.
And what does Mother do?
Lay out the money.
And what does the baby do?
Eat up the honey.

Q: Why did Fido beat up Rover?
A: Because Rover was a boxer.

Q: What do you get when an elephant sneezes?
A: You get out of the way!

Q: What kind of animal do you take into battle?
A: An army-dillo.

Q: What kind of bird likes to make bread?
A: The dodo bird (dough-dough).

Q: What do you get when your dog makes your breakfast?
A: You get pooched eggs.

Q: Why did the horse wake up with a headache?
A: Because at bedtime he hit the hay.

Q: What do trees and dogs have in common?
A: They both have bark.

Q: Why do bumblebees smell so good?
A: They always wear bee-odorant.

Q: What do you get if you mix a rabbit and a snake?
A: A jump rope.

Q: Why was the Tyrannosaurus rex so boring?
A: He was a dino-snore.

Q: What is a frog's favorite drink?
A: Croak-a-Cola.

Q: What is the scariest kind of bug?
A: A zom-bee (zombie).

Q: What do you call a lazy kangaroo?
A: A pouch potato.

Q: What happened when the sharks raced each other?
A: They tide (get it . . . they tied).

Q: Why couldn't the goats get along?
A: They kept butting heads.

Q: What kind of bats are silly?
A: Ding-bats.

Q: Why are frogs so happy?
A: They just eat whatever bugs them!

Q: What is the difference between a fish and a piano?
A: You can't tuna fish (tune a fish).

Q: What did the horse say when he tripped and fell down?
A: "Help! I've fallen and I can't giddy-up!"

Q: If people like sandwiches, what do lions like?
A: Man-wiches.

Q: When do fireflies get stressed out?
A: When they need to lighten up!

Q: Why do rhinos have so many wrinkles?
A: Because they're so hard to iron.

Q: **Where did the turtle fill up his gas tank?**
A: At the shell station.

Q: **Why did the pony get sent to his room without supper?**
A: He wouldn't stop horsing around.

Q: **Why did the chicken cross the road?**
A: To show the squirrel it could be done.

Q: **Why did the turkey cross the road?**
A: To prove it wasn't a chicken.

Q: **What do you give a horse with a bad cold?**
A: Cough stirrup.

Q: **Who falls asleep at a bullfight?**
A: A bull-dozer.

Q: What is a snake's favorite subject in school?
A. World hissstory.

Q: What do you get when you cross a goat and a computer?
A: A ram.

Q: What do you call an insect that complains all the time?
A: A grumble-bee.

Q: Why were the deer, the chipmunk, and the squirrel laughing so hard?
A: Because the owl was a hoot!

Q: Why did the cat and her kittens clean up their mess?
A: They didn't want to litter.

Q: **What is a sheep's favorite kind of food?**
A: Bah-bah-cue.

Q: **What is a hyena's favorite kind of candy?**
A: A Snickers bar.

Q: **How do sea creatures communicate under water?**
A: With shell phones.

Q: **What do you call a monkey who won't behave?**
A: A bad-boon.

Q: **What kind of bugs read the dictionary?**
A: Spelling bees.

Q: **What do you call a calf that gets into trouble?**
A: Ground-ed beef.

Q: What do you call a dinosaur who's scared all the time?
A: A nervous rex.

Q: What do you call a polar bear in Hawaii?
A: Lost!

Q: Why was the dog depressed?
A: Because his life was so ruff.

Q: What does a rabbit use to fix its fur?
A: Hare-spray.

Q: What kind of insect is hard to understand?
A: A mumble-bee.

Q: Where do you take a hornet when it's sick?
A: To the wasp-ital (hospital).

Q: Who made the fish's wish come true?
A: Its fairy cod-mother.

Q: Where do pigs like to take a nap?
A: In their ham-mock.

Q: What do you call a cow that can't give milk?
A: A milk dud.

Q: Why did the chickens get in trouble at school?
A: They were using fowl language.

Q: Where does a lizard keep his groceries?
A: In the refriger-gator.

Q: Why is talking to cows a waste of time?
A: Whatever you say goes in one ear and out the udder.

Q: What do you get if a cow is in an earthquake?
A: A milkshake.

Q: How does a farmer count his cattle?
A: With a cow-culator.

Q: Why does a milking stool have only three legs?
A: Because the cow has the udder one.

Q: Where do rabbits go after their wedding?
A: They go on their bunny-moon.

Q: What do you get when you cross a dog with a cell phone?
A: A golden receiver.

Q: Where did the bull take the cow on a date?
A: To dinner and a mooovie.

Q: What is the world's hungriest animal?
A: A turkey—it just gobble, gobble, gobbles!

Joe: There were ten cats on a boat and one jumped off. How many were left?
Jack: I don't know, Joe. I guess nine?
Joe: No, there were none! They were all a bunch of copycats.

Q: How come hyenas are so healthy?
A: Because laughter is the best medicine.

Q: Why don't dalmatians like to take baths?
A: They don't like to be spotless.

Q: What do you get when sheep do karate?
A: Lamb chops.

Q: What happened to the mouse when it fell in the bathtub?
A: It came out squeaky clean.

Q: Why did the cowboy ask his cattle so many questions?
A: He wanted to grill them.

Q: What is a duck's favorite snack?
A: Cheese and quackers.

Q: What do you call a cow that's afraid of everything?
A: A cow-ard.

Q: Why did the rooster go to the doctor?
A: It had the cock-a-doodle-flu.

Q: How do birds get ready to work out?
A: They do their worm-ups.

Q: What kind of insects are bad at football?
A: Fumblebees.

Q: What do you call a deer with no eyes?
A: No eye deer (no idea).

Q: Why is it so easy for an elephant to get a job?
A: Because they'll work for peanuts.

Q: What is the difference between a cat and a frog?
A: A cat has nine lives but a frog croaks every day.

Q: What does a frog say when he washes windows?
A: "Rubbit, rubbit, rubbit."

Q: What do you get when a lion escapes from the zoo?
A: A cat-astrophe.

Q: What is the best kind of cat to have around?
A: A dandy-lion.

Q: What did the tiger say to her cubs when they wanted to go out and play?
A: "Be careful—it's a jungle out there!"

Q: Why did the monkey almost get fired?
A: It took him awhile to get in the swing of things.

Q: Why are snails one of the strongest creatures in the world?
A: They can carry their house on their back.

Q: What do you get when you cross a bear with a forest?
A: You get fur trees.

Q: Where do trout keep their money?
A: In a river bank.

Q: What did the worm say to her daughter when she came home late?

A: "Where on earth have you been?"

Q: What did the boy say when he threw a slug across the room?

A: "Man, how slime flies!"

Q: Why did the elephant cross the road?

A: It's an elephant, so who's going to stop him?

Q: What is a frog's favorite flower?

A: A croak-us (crocus).

Q: How do you keep a dog from barking in the back seat of the car?

A: Put him in the front seat of the car.

Q: What do you get when you cross a monkey and a peach?
A: You get an ape-ricot.

Q: How do you greet a frog?
A: "Wart's up?"

Q: What do you get when you cross Bambi with an umbrella?
A: You get a rain-deer (reindeer).

Q: Who brings kittens for Christmas?
A: Santa Claws.

Where Do Animals Come From?

Bees come from Sting-apore

Cows come from Moo-rocco

Fish come from Wales

Sharks come from Finland

Ants come from Frants (France)

Dogs come from Bark-celona
   (Barcelona)

Pigs come from New Ham-shire

Chickens come from Turkey

Cats come from Purrr-u (Peru)

Birds come from Air-azona

Sheep come from the Baa-hamas

Snakes come from Hiss-issippi

Q: What did Santa give Rudolph for his upset stomach?
A: Elk-A-Seltzer

Q: Why can't an elephant's trunk be 12 inches long?
A: Because then it would be a foot.

Q: What do you get when you cross a fish and a tree branch?
A: A fish stick.

Q: What kind of bird is always depressed?
A: A bluebird.

Q: How high can a bumblebee count?
A: To a buzz-illion.

Q: Why are oysters so strong?
A: Because of their mussels (muscles).

Q: **What do you get when you throw a pony in the ocean?**
A: A seahorse!

Q: **What is the most colorful kind of snake in the world?**
A: A rain-boa constrictor (rainbow).

Q: **What does a cow keep in its wallet?**
A: Moo-la.

Q: **What kind of fish comes out at night?**
A: A starfish.

Q: **What did the dog say to its owner?**
A: "I woof you."

Q: Why couldn't the dog visit the psychiatrist?
A: Because it wasn't allowed on the couch.

Q: What kind of cats like to play in the water?
A: Sea lions.

Knock, knock!
Who's there?
Moo.
Moo, who?
Make up your mind—are you a cow or an owl?

Q: How does a dog say goodbye?
A: "Bone-Voyage!"

Q: What do llamas like to drink?
A: Strawberry llama-nade (lemonade).

Q: What do you call a fish with no eyes?
A: Fsh!

Q: What do you get when you throw a pig into the bushes?
A: A hedgehog.

Did You Know · · ·

A hedgehog's heart beats 300 times per minute.

Q: **What did the duck say to the clerk at the store?**
A: "Just put it on my bill!"

Q: **What did the frogs say to each other on their wedding day?**
A: "I'll love you until the day I croak!"

Q: **Why was the golden retriever so stressed out?**
A: Because he has so doggone much to do.

Q: **Why was the horse in so much pain?**
A: Because he was a charlie horse.

Q: **What is red and weights 14,000 pounds?**
A: An elephant holding its breath.

Q: **What do cats like to eat for a snack?**
A: Mice krispy bars.

Did You Know . . .

A butterfly's tastebuds are in its feet.

Q: How did the bunny rabbit feel when he ran out of carrots?
A: It made him unhoppy!

Q: What does a hen do when she goes grocery shopping?
A: She makes a list and chicks it twice!

Q: What did the fish say when it won the prize?
A: "That's fin-tastic (fantastic)!"

Q: Why did the grizzly tell the same story over and over?
A: Because he said it *bears* repeating!

Q: What will a moose do if he calls when you're not home?
A: He'll leave a detailed moose-age.

Q: What do you get when you put glasses on a pony?
A: A see-horse.

Q: Where do bunnies like to eat?
A: IHOP!

Q: How do you know when a rhino is ready to charge?
A: It gets out its credit card.

Knock, knock!
Who's there?
Raymond.
Raymond who?
Raymond me to take the dog for a walk!

Q: What do you call a racoon that crosses the road with his eyes shut?
A: Roadkill!

Q: Where should a 600-pound lion go?
A: On a diet!

Q: How do you keep a skunk from smelling?
A: Hold its nose!

Q: What do you get when you cross a bear with a skunk?
A: Winnie the Pew.

Q: What kind of sea creature is always depressed?
A: A blue whale.

Q: What did the beaver say to the tree?
A: "It's been nice getting to gnaw you! "

Q: What did the roach wear to the party?
A: A cock-broach.

Q: Why was the dog hungry all the time?
A: Because it was a chow.

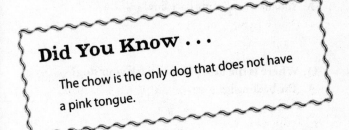

Did You Know · · ·

The chow is the only dog that does not have a pink tongue.

Q: **What kind of animal wears shoes while it's sleeping?**

A: A horse!

Q: **Why did the gum cross the road?**

A: Because it was stuck to the chicken's shoe!

Q: **How does a mother hen know when her chicks are ready to hatch?**

A: She uses an egg timer.

Q: **What happens when you get a thousand bunnies to line up and jump backward?**

A: You have a receding hare line!

Q: **Where is the best place to park your dog?**

A: The barking lot.

Q: What do you get when a cat climbs down your chimney with a bag of presents?
A: Santa Paws.

Q: Why can't you hear a dinosaur talk?
A: Because dinosaurs are extinct!

Q: Why don't lobsters share their toys?
A: Because they're shellfish (selfish)!

Knock, knock!
Who's there?
Either.
Either who?
It's the Either Bunny!

Q: What is a chicken's favorite composer?
A: Bach, Bach, Bach!

Q: **What is a fly's favorite composer?**
A: Shoo-bert (Schubert).

Q: **What do you get when you cross a bat and a cell phone?**
A: A bat-mobile.

Q: **Did you know that a kangaroo can jump higher than your house?**
A: Of course! Your house can't jump!

Q: **What time does a duck get up?**
A: At the quack of dawn.

Q: **What is black, white, and wet all over?**
A: A zebra that was pushed into a swimming pool!

Q: What's black, white, and laughing?
A: The zebra that pushed the other zebra into the swimming pool!

Q: Why don't bunnies tell scary stories?
A: Because it makes the hare stand up on the back of their necks.

Q: What do you call a man with a seagull on his head?
A: Cliff.

Q: What do you call a monkey in a minefield?
A: A ba-BOOM!

Q: What do you call a pig that took a plane?
A: Swine flew (flu).

Q: What was the elephant doing on the freeway?
A: I don't know—about 10 miles per hour?

Jack: Do you like that cow over there?
Jill: No, I like the udder one!

Did You Know . . .

An ostrich's eye is bigger than its brain.

Q: What do cats use to do their homework?
A: A meow-culator.

Q: Why did the hornet have to fly back home?
A: Because he forgot his yellow jacket.

Q: Why did the bee visit the barber?
A: Because he wanted a buzz cut.

Bill: Would you like some honey?
Bob: May-bee!

Q: How did the bee get ready for school?
A: She used her honey comb!

Q: What do you get when you cross a vulture and a bumblebee?
A: A buzz-ard.

Q: What is a horse's favorite kind of fruit?
A: Straw-berries.

Q: What is a horse's favorite kind of nut?
A: Hay-zelnuts.

Q: What is a mouse's favorite game?
A: Hide and squeak.

Q: Why do birds fly south for the winter?
A: Because it's too far to walk, and their feet won't reach the pedals on a bicycle!

Cow #1: Did you hear about that crazy disease going around called mad cow disease?
Cow #2: I sure did—good thing I'm a penguin!

A policeman saw a lady with a hippopotamus walking down the street. He said, "Ma'am, you need to take that hippo to the zoo." The next day the lady was again walking down the street with the hippopotamus. The policeman said, "Ma'am, I told you to take that hippo to the zoo." The lady replied, "I did take him to the zoo, and today I'm taking him to the movies!"

Q: What is the best way to communicate with a squirrel?
A: Climb up a tree and act like a nut!

Q: Why can't cats drink milk in outer space?
A: Because the milk is in flying saucers!

Q: What's more annoying than a cat meowing outside your bedroom window?
A: *Ten* cats meowing outside your bedroom window!

Q: What do you do when you come upon two snails fighting?
A: Just let them slug it out . . .

Q: What's the best way to learn about spiders?
A: On a web-site!

Q: What does a frog drink when it wants to lose weight?
A: Diet Croak.

Q: **Why did the firefly get bad grades on his report card?**
A: Because he wasn't very bright!

Q: **Why was the caterpillar running for its life?**
A: Because it was being chased by a dog-erpillar!

Did You Know . . .

The golden poison dart frog is one of the most poisonous animals on earth. A single two-inch frog has enough venom to kill ten grown men.

www.nationalgeographic.com

The Caterpillar
Christina Rosetti

Caterpillar
Brown and furry
Caterpillar in a hurry,
Take a walk
To the shady lead, or stalk,
Or what not,
Which may be the chosen spot.
No toad spy you,
Hovering bird of prey pass by you;
Spin and die,
To live again a butterfly.

Q: What do you get when you cross a dog and a snowman?

A: Frostbite.

Q: What is the difference between a fly and an eagle?

A: An eagle can fly, but a fly can't eagle.

Q: When is it bad luck to see a black cat?

A: When you're a mouse!

A duck went shopping at the grocery story and went to the register to pay. The store clerk asked, "Don't you have exact change?" The duck answered, "Nope, sorry, I only carry bills!"

Q: What do you call an elephant that never takes a bath?

A: A smell-ephant!

Q: What is a fish's favorite game show?
A: Name that tuna (tune).

Knock, knock!
Who's there?
Bee.
Bee who?
Just bee yourself!

Knock, knock!
Who's there?
Owl.
Owl who?
Owl tell you another joke if you let me in . . .

Knock, knock!
Who's there?
Aardvark.
Aardvark who?
Aardvark a thousand miles just to see you!

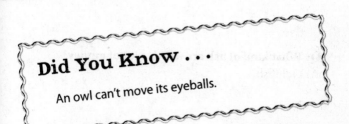

Did You Know · · ·

An owl can't move its eyeballs.

Knock, knock!
Who's there?
Amos.
Amos who?
Ouch! Amos-quito bit me!

Knock, knock!
Who's there?
Bug spray.
Bug spray who?
Bug spray they won't get squished!

Q: Where do horses live?
A: In neigh-borhoods.

Q: What kind of fish are worth a lot of money?
A: Goldfish.

Q: Where do monkeys make their burgers?
A: On the grill-a (gorilla).

Q: What did one nightcrawler say to the other nightcrawler?
A: "I know this great place down the road where we can eat dirt cheap!"

Q: Why does a herd of deer have plenty of money?
A: Because they have a lot of bucks!

Q: What is a bug's favorite music?
A: The Beatles.

Q: What is a frogs favorite outdoor game?
A: Croak-quet (croquet)

Q: What kind of animal will never leave you alone?
A: The badger.

Q: Why did the bug get up early every morning?
A: Because it was a praying mantis.

Q: What kind of animal always contradicts itself?
A: A hippo-crite.

Q: Where do you put your dog when he's not behaving?
A: In the grrrrr-age!

Q: What do you call a cat with eight legs that can swim?
A: An octo-puss.

Q: Why were the robins eating cake?
A: Because it was their bird-thday!

Q: Why did the pythons decide to get married?
A: Because they had a crush on each other.

Q: What do you do if there is a lion in your bed?
A: Go to a hotel for the night!

Q: What do you get when you cross a snail and a porcupine?
A: A slow poke.

Q: What's green, has six legs, and climbs bean-stalks?
A: The Jolly Green Gi-ant.

Q: What's gray and goes round and round and round?

A: An elephant on a merry-go-round.

Q: Why did the raccoon cross the road twice?
A: Because it was a double crosser.

Q: What do you get when you have a bunch of giraffes on the highway?
A: A giraff-ic jam.

Q: What performs at the circus and flies around eating mosquitos?
A: An acro-bat.

Q: Why was the crow on the phone?
A: Because he was making a long-distance phone caw!

Customer: Do you serve turkeys here?
Waitress: We serve anyone, so go ahead and take a seat.

Q: How do fleas travel from dog to dog?
A: By itch hiking.

Did You Know · · ·

A bat lives about 40 years.

Knock, knock!
Who's there?
Gnat.
Gnat who?
I'm gnat who you think I am!

Knock, knock!
Who's there?
Moose.
Moose who?
It moose be time to let me in, so open the door!

Q: How do you know which end of a worm is the head?

A: Tickle the middle and see which end laughs.

Q: Why are chickens so bad at baseball?

A: Because they're always hitting fowl balls.

Q: What do you get when you cross a beetle and a rabbit?

A: Bugs bunny!

Q: What do skunks like to eat when they're hungry?

A: Peanut butter and smelly sandwiches.

Q: What do you get when you cross a penguin and a jalapeño?

A: A chilly pepper.

Q: Why can't you trust what a pig says?
A: Because it's full of bologna.

Q: What's large, gray, and has eighteen wheels?
A: An elephant in a semi-truck.

Q: What is a polar bear's favorite breakfast?
A: Ice krispies.

Q: Why did all the animals fall asleep in the barn?
A: Because the pigs were so boar-ing (boring).

Q: Why didn't the snake know how much it weighed?
A: Because it shed its scales.

Q: What does a leopard say after dinner?
A: "That hit the spot!"

Q: How does a cow get to church on Sunday?
A: On its moo-torcycle.

Q: Why did the moose lift weights at the gym?
A: Because it wanted big moose-les (muscles).

Q: Why didn't the crab spend any of his money?
A: Because he was a penny pincher.

Q: What does a cow like to drink before bed?
A: De-calf-inated coffee (decaffeinated).

Q: What are you doing if you're staring at a starfish?
A: Stargazing.

Q: Why was the duck happy after his doctor's appointment?
A: Because he got a clean bill of health.

Q: Where do bugs go to do their shopping?
A: The flea market.

Q: What kind of dessert do dogs run away from?
A: Pound cake.

Q: How do you know if there is a black bear in your oven?
A: The oven door won't close!

Q: Why did the cheetah get glasses?
A: Because it was seeing spots.

Knock, knock!
Who's there?
Cod.
Cod who?
Cod you let me in? It's cold out here!

Knock, knock!
Who's there?
Shellfish.
Shellfish who?
Don't be shellfish—let me in!

Knock, knock!
Who's there?
Rhino.
Rhino who?
Rhino you want to let me in.

Knock, knock!
Who's there?
Raven.
Raven who?
I've been raven about you to all my friends, so won't you let me in?

Q: What is the richest bird in the world?
A: The golden eagle.

Q: Why was a pig on the airplane?
A: Because its owner wanted to see pigs fly.

Q: Why was the frog in a bad mood?
A: Because he was having a toad-ally bad day.

Q: What do you call an elephant in a phone booth?
A: Stuck!

Q: Why were the elephants kicked off the beach?
A: Because they kept throwing their trunks in the water.

Q: Where do old ants go?
A: The ant-ique store.

Q: What do you get when you cross a cow and a toad?
A: A bullfrog.

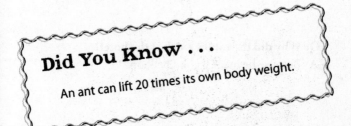

Did You Know . . .

An ant can lift 20 times its own body weight.

Q: What do you get when you cross a water buffalo and a chicken?

A: Soggy buffalo wings.

Q: How do chickens stay in shape?

A: They eggs-ercise.

Q: How do skunks watch the news?
A: On their smell-evision.

Q: Why did the rabbit work at the hotel?
A: Because he made a good bellhop.

Josh: How do you know carrots are good for your eyes?
Anna: Have you ever seen a rabbit wearing glasses?

Q: What do dinosaurs put in their cars?
A: Fossil fuel.

Q: How did the pig write a letter?
A: With its pig pen.

Rob Elliott

What's Their Motto?

Bee: Mind your own beeswax.

Bear: Grin and bear it.

Cow: Keep moooooving.

Dog: Don't bark up the wrong tree.

Owl: It's not what you know, it's WHO you know.

Rabbit: Don't worry, be hoppy.

Cat: Don't litter.

Mouse: The squeaky wheel gets the grease.

Bat: Just fang in there.

Otter: Do unto otters as you would have them do unto you.

Robin: The early bird gets the worm.

Fox: Don't count your chickens before they're hatched.

Fish: Absence makes the heart grow flounder.

83

Q: What happened to the snake when it got upset?
A: It got hiss-terical.

Q: What did the rattlesnakes do after they had a fight?
A: They hissed and made up.

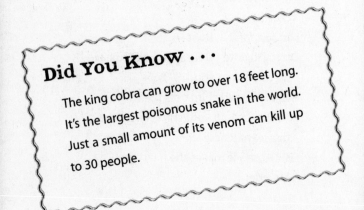

Did You Know . . .

The king cobra can grow to over 18 feet long. It's the largest poisonous snake in the world. Just a small amount of its venom can kill up to 30 people.

Q: What does a monkey drink with its breakfast?
A: Ape juice.

Q: What happened to the platypus when it fell in the hole?
A: It became a splatypus.

Did You Know . . .

The duckbill platypus can store over 500 worms in its cheeks.

Q: How do crocodiles make their dinner?
A: In a croc pot.

Q: Where do ants go when it's hot outside?
A: Ant-arctica.

Q: Why do pigs make great comedians?
A: Because they like to ham it up.

Q: What is a pig's favorite play?
A: Hamlet.

Q: Where do pigs put their dirty laundry?
A: In the hamper.

Q: Why was the pig having trouble walking?
A: Because he pulled his hamstring.

Q: What do you get if you cross a dog and a mosquito?
A: A bloodhound.

Q: What do you get when you combine a cat and a dog?
A: Catnip.

Q: What does a squirrel like to eat for breakfast?
A: Dough-nuts!

Q: What is a monkey's favorite book?
A: Apes of Wrath.

Q: How do skunks get in touch with each other?
A: They use their smell phones.

Q: How do crabs call each other?
A: They use their shell phones.

Q: What do you call a ladybug that won't clean up
   its room?

A: A litterbug.

Knock, knock!
Who's there?
Otter.
Otter who?
You otter open this door and let me in!

Knock, knock!
Who's there?
Dragon.
Dragon who?
Quit dragon this out and open the door!

Q: What happened to the rich snake who had
   everything?

A: He decided to scale back.

Q: How do you stop a 10-pound parrot from talking too much?

A: Buy a 20-pound cat.

Q: Why did the cat study its spelling words fifty times?

A: Because practice makes purr-fect.

At the Zoo
William Makepeace Thackeray

First I saw the white bear, then I
 saw the black;
Then I saw the camel with a
 hump upon his back;
Then I saw the grey wolf, with
 mutton in his maw;
Then I saw the wombat waddle in
 the straw;
Then I saw the elephant a-waving
 of his trunk;
Then I saw the monkeys—mercy,
 how unpleasantly they smelt!

Q: What do you get when you cross a brontosaurus and a lemon?
A: A dino-sour.

Q: What's green, has warts, and lives alone?
A: Hermit the frog.

Q: Why was the bird wearing a wig?
A: Because it was a bald eagle.

Q: What did the baby shark do when it got lost in the ocean?
A: It whaled (wailed).

Q: What kind of house does a pig live in?
A: A hog cabin.

Q: How do frogs send a telegraph?
A: They use Morse toad (code).

Q: How did the frog get over the tall wall?
A: With a tad-pole.

Q: What is a cow's favorite vegetable?
A: Cow-iflower.

Q: Why did the pigs write a lot of letters?
A: Because they were pen pals.

Q: What does a cat wear at night?
A: Its paw-jamas.

Q: What did the night crawler's parents say after their child got home after curfew?
A: "Where on earth have you been?"

Ode to a Cricket
Virginia Satterfield Totsch

Little cricket is up at dawn
Getting dressed, has one shoe on
Little Annie Dachshund came out to play
And she spied Mr. Cricket right away!
Run cricket run
Annie will get you
Cricket ran, cricket flew
Cricket lost his little shoe
Doesn't matter, come what may
Annie got him anyway!

Q: Where did the fish go each morning?
A: To their school.

Q: What does a racehorse like to eat for lunch?
A: Fast food.

Q: What do you give a mouse on its birthday?
A: Cheese-cake.

Knock, knock!
Who's there?
Iguana.
Iguana who?
Iguana come in, so please open up!

**Emma: If Noah got milk from the cows, eggs from
the chickens, and wool from the sheep on the
ark, what did he get from the ducks?**
Leah: I don't know, Emma, what?
Emma: Quackers!

Q: Which animal on the ark had the highest IQ?
A: The giraffe!

Q: What do you get when you pour boiling water down a rabbit hole?
A: Hot Cross Bunnies.

Knock, knock!
Who's there?
Owl.
Owl who?
I'm tired of knocking, so owl see you later.

Q: What do cobras put on their bathroom floor?
A: Rep-tiles.

Q: What's a cow's favorite painting?
A: The Moo-na Lisa.

Q: What is a bee's favorite toy?
A: A fris-bee!

Q: What is a dolphin's favorite game show?
A: Whale of Fortune.

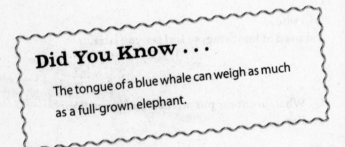

Did You Know · · ·

The tongue of a blue whale can weigh as much as a full-grown elephant.

Q: What does a goat use when it's camping?
A: A sheeping bag.

Q: What kind of dog is good at chemistry?
A: A Lab-rador retriever.

Q: What is a lightning bug's favorite game?
A: Hide and glow seek.

Q: Why did the cat go to the beauty salon?
A: It needed a pet-icure.

Q: How did the leopard lose its spots?
A: It took a bath and came out spotless.

Q: What did the firefly say before the big race?
A: "Ready, set, glow!"

Q: What did the firefly have for lunch?
A: A light meal.

Q: What did the wolf say when it met its new neighbors?
A: "Howl are you doing?"

Q: Why don't goats mind their own business?
A: Because they're always butting in.

Q: What did the mother possum say to her son?
A: "Quit hanging around all day and do something!"

Q: Why did the cat vanish into thin air?
A: Because it drank evaporated milk.

Q: Where do cows go to dance?
A: The meatball.

Knock, knock!
Who's there?
Seal.
Seal who?
My lips are sealed until you open the door!

Q: What lives in a hole, has horns, and runs really fast?

A: An ant-elope.

Q: What kind of tree has the most bark?

A: The dogwood tree.

Q: Why didn't the bug feel like doing anything?

A: Because it was a slug.

Q: What's a bird's favorite movie?

A: Batman and Robin.

Q: What happened to the worm when it didn't clean its room?

A: It was grounded.

Q: Why did the cat have trouble using its computer?

A: Because it kept eating the mouse.

Q: Why did the mosquito wake up in the middle of the night?
A: It was having a bite-mare.

Knock, knock!
Who's there?
Goat.
Goat who?
You're getting my goat—just let me in!

Q: What is a wolf's favorite treat?
A: Pigs in a blanket.

Q: What is a wolf's favorite book?
A: Little Howl on the Prairie.

Q: What did the bird wear to the ball?
A: A duck-sedo (tuxedo).

Q: **Why did the dinosaur cross the road?**
A: To eat the chickens on the other side.

Q: **When can an elephant sit under an umbrella and not get wet?**
A: When it's not raining.

Q: **What is the sleepiest dinosaur?**
A: The Bronto-snore-ous.

Q: **What do you get when a rhinoceros goes running through your garden?**
A: Squash.

Q: **Why did the dog quit playing football?**
A: The game got too ruff (rough).

Q: **What do you get when you cross a pig and a cow?**
A: A ham-burger.

Q: What do you do if a cow won't give milk?
A: You mooove on to the udder one.

Q: Why did the horse wake up in the middle of the night?
A: It was having a night-mare.

Q: What do you get when a pig does karate?
A: Pork chops!

Q: Where do cats shop for their toys?
A: From a toy cat-alog.

Q: How are A's just like flowers?
A: Bees follow them.

Q: Where do fish like to sleep?
A: On their water beds.

Q: What kind of birds like to stick together?
A: Vel-crows.

Q: What do you get when you cross a salmon and an elephant?
A: Swim trunks.

Q: What is a frog's favorite snack?
A: French flies.

Q: What is big, gray, and wears glass slippers?
A: Cinderelephant.

Q: Why do fish make good lawyers?
A. Because they like de-bait.

Q: What do you get when a barn full of cows won't give milk?
A: Udder chaos.

Q: What do you call it when one cow is spying on another cow?
A: A steak out.

Tim: My dog keeps chasing people on a bike!
Tom: Why don't you put him on a leash?
Tim: No, I think I'll just take his bike away.

Q: What's a cow's favorite game?
A: Moo-sical chairs.

Q: What kind of keys never unlock anything?
A: Monkeys, turkeys, and donkeys.

Jill: How do elephants smell?
Jane: Not very good!

Q: What has two heads, four eyes, six legs, and a tail?
A: A cowboy on a horse.

Q: Where do bears keep their clothes?
A: In a claw-set (closet).

Q: What kind of bugs wear sneakers?
A: Shoo flies (shoe flies).

Q: What game do leopards always lose?
A: Hide and seek—they always get spotted.

Q: Why are snails shy at parties?
A: They don't want to come out of their shell.

Q: Why did the bull owe so much money?
A: Because it always charged.

Q: What is a chicken's favorite game?
A: Duck, duck, goose.

Q: Did you hear about the dog that didn't have any teeth?
A: Its bark was worse than its bite.

Q: What do dogs have that no other animals have?
A: Puppies.

Knock, knock!
Who's there?
Fur.
Fur who?
I'm waiting fur you to open the door!

Q: What has a horn but does not honk?
A: A rhinoceros.

Q: Why do dragons sleep all day?
A: Because they like to hunt knights.

Q: What kind of bone is hard for a dog to eat?
A: A trombone.

Did you know · · ·

There are only two types of egg-laying mammals: the duck-billed platypus and the echidna (also known as the spiny anteater). Both are only found in Australia and New Guinea.

Q: How did the gorilla fix its bike?
A: With a monkey wrench.

Q: What is a woodpecker's favorite kind of joke?
A: A knock-knock joke.

Q: What do you call a story about a giraffe?
A: A tall tale.

Q: What did the vet give to the sick parakeet?
A: A special tweetment.

Anna: Can a seagull eat fifty fish in an hour?
Leah: No, but a peli-can!

Q: What kind of bee is good for your health?
A: Vitamin B.

Q: What do you get when you put a pig in a blender?
A: Bacon bits.

Q: Why do elephants have trunks?
A: Because they would look silly with suitcases.

Q: What kind of dogs can tell time?
A: Watchdogs.

Q: What do you get when you combine a bear and a pig?
A: A teddy boar.

Q: How did the bird open the can of birdseed?
A: With a crowbar.

Two cockroaches are eating together in a garbage can. One cockroach says to the other, "Did you hear about the new restaurant that opened up down the road? It has the cleanest kitchen I've ever seen. The place sparkles and shines. There isn't a crumb anywhere to be found!" The other cockroach looked up and said, "Please stop! I'm eating here!"

Q: What do woodpeckers eat for breakfast?
A: Oak-meal.

Q: How do dolphins make hard decisions?
A: By flippering a coin.

Q: Why was the lion always tired?
A: It would only take catnaps.

Q: What is the smartest bird in the world?
A: Owl-bert Einstein.

Q: What kind of animal never gets old?
A: A gnu (new).

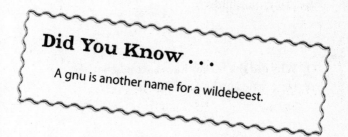

Did You Know . . .

A gnu is another name for a wildebeest.

Q: How do turkeys travel across the ocean?
A: In a gravy boat.

Q: What did the wolf do when he heard the joke?
A: He howled.

Q: What did the spider say to the fly?
A: "Why don't you stick around for a while?"

Q: How do you grow a blackbird?
A: Plant some birdseed.

Q: Why did the turkey have a stomachache?
A: He gobbled up his food too fast.

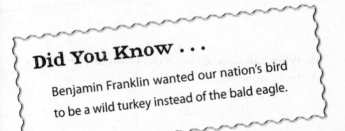

Did You Know . . .

Benjamin Franklin wanted our nation's bird to be a wild turkey instead of the bald eagle.

Knock, knock!
Who's there?
Bat.
Bat who?
I bat you're going to let me in soon!

Q: What did the mouse say when he lost his piece of cheese?
A: "Rats!"

Q: **What is a cat's favorite dessert?**
A: Mice cream.

Q: **Where do skunks like to sit in church?**
A: In the front pew.

Josh: Should I go see the prairie dogs in Texas?
Anna: Sure, Josh, gopher it!

Q: **What do you get when you cross a deer and a pirate?**
A: A buck-aneer.

Q: **Why was the elephant mad at the bellman?**
A: He dropped its trunk.

Q: **What happened when the giraffes had a race?**
A: They were neck and neck the whole time.

Q: Why didn't the llama get any dessert?
A: He wouldn't eat his llama beans (lima beans).

**Q: What does a cat do when he wants popcorn in
the middle of the movie?**
A: He pushes the paws button.

Knock, knock!
Who's there?
Elephant.
Elephant who?
You forgot to feed the elephant?!

Knock, knock!
Who's there?
Badger.
Badger who?
I'll stop badgering you if you let me in!

Q: **What do polar bears eat for lunch?**
A: Iceberg-ers.

Q: **How can you tell if a moose has been in your freezer?**
A: By the moose tracks.

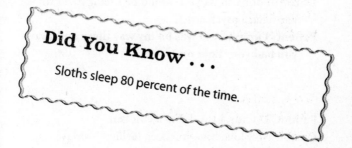

Did You Know . . .

Sloths sleep 80 percent of the time.

Q: What did one cat say to the other cat?
A: "Can you hear me meow?"

Knock, knock!
Who's there?
Lion.
Lion who?
Quit lion around and answer the door already!

Patient: Doctor, I have a problem. I think I'm a moth.

Doctor: I don't think you should be seeing me. I think you need a psychiatrist!

Patient: I know, but I was on my way there and I saw you had your light on.

Patient: Doctor, I think I'm a chicken.

Doctor: How long have you been feeling this way?

Patient: Ever since I was a little egg.

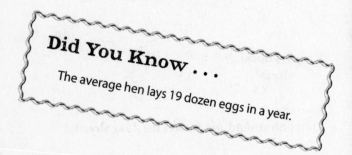

Did You Know . . .

The average hen lays 19 dozen eggs in a year.

Silly Animal Tongue Twisters

(Say these three times as fast as you can!)

Kitty catty, paws, claws, mouse,
house, whiskers, tricksters,
fur, purr, pounce!

Purple penguins play ping-pong.

Bullfrogs blow big bubbles.

Sneaky snakes slither slowly.

Big bears bounce balls.

Skinks think skunks stink.

Beefy blazing bison burgers.

Moths thought sloths got flaws.

ROB ELLIOTT has been a publishing professional for more than fifteen years and lives in West Michigan, where in his spare time he enjoys laughing out loud with his wife and four children.

Need More Laughs?

- - - - - - - -   - - - - - - - - -

Visit

LOLJokesForKids.com

to submit your own jokes,
receive FREE printable doodle pages,
and watch the video!

• • •

f *Laugh-Out-Loud Jokes for Kids*

🐦 *@loljokesforkids*

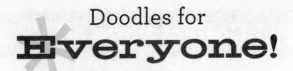

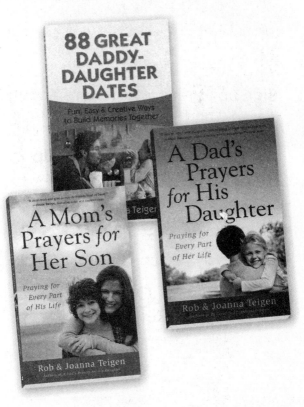